YOU Can Do Anything!

40 Inspirational Activities

ARCTURUS

ARCTURUS

This edition published in 2022 by Arcturus Publishing Limited
26/27 Bickels Yard, 151–153 Bermondsey Street,
London SE1 3HA

Authors: Anna Claybourne, Claudia Martin, and Thomas Canavan
Illustrators: Ocean Hughes and Katie Kear
Editors: Lucy Doncaster, Kait Eaton, Donna Gregory, Stephanie Carey,
  and Violet Peto
Designers: Lucy Doncaster, Duck Egg Blue, Jeni Child,
  and Sarah Fountain
Art Direction: Rosie Bellwood
Consultants: Dr. Emma Watson, Dougal Dixon, Sarah Ackland,
  Nina Ridge, and Jules Howard

ISBN: 978-1-3988-1990-0
CH010342NT
Supplier 29, Date 0422, PI 00000971

Printed in China

What is STEM?

STEM is a world-wide initiative that aims to cultivate an interest in Science, Technology, Engineering, and Mathematics, in an effort to promote these disciplines to as wide a variety of students as possible.

PLEASE NOTE:
The medical content of this book is not intended to be a substitute for professional medical advice. Always seek the advice of a qualified health provider if you have any health concerns.

Contents

You Can Be Anything You Want to Be!

Have you ever thought about what you would like to be when you grow up? Maybe you are passionate about the planet and want to be an eco-scientist, are intrigued by the human body and plan to be a doctor, or else you dream of going into space and hope to be a rocket scientist or astronaut. Or perhaps you aren't sure yet, and want to consider lots of options before you decide.

Whatever stage you are at, this book can help. It takes a look at a wide range of careers, explaining what the job involves, what you might need to be good at or interested in, and the sorts of tasks you might carry out. What's more, it's packed with loads of fascinating facts and inspirational stories, as well as activities, puzzles, games, and quizzes. The answers for these can be found on pages 90–91.

So, open your mind, grab a pencil and a piece of paper, and prepare to explore the limitless opportunities out there. Who knows—maybe in the future you could be the one to come up with a solution to climate change, make the next major medical breakthrough, or crack a big criminal case!

You Can Be a Rocket Scientist

Do you want to learn about rocket science? "Rocket science" is often used to mean really hard science. In fact, the way rockets work is quite simple. When a rocket takes off, gas and flames shoot out of the bottom. As the rocket pushes them out, they push back. That's what makes it go.

Science genius Isaac Newton summed it up in 1686, when he said ...

Fuel burning inside the rocket makes the gas shoot out.

Rocket pushes the gas down.

Gas pushes the rocket up.

The force that makes the rocket go is called thrust.

"... for every action, there is an equal and opposite reaction!"

What Newton meant was simpler than it sounds. When one thing pushes on another, an equal force pushes back.

Activity: Rocket Balloon

This rocket balloon works the same way, except that it uses air instead of burning gas.

You will need:

- A piece of string about 3 m (10 feet) long
- A drinking straw
- A balloon
- Tape
- Scissors

1. Tie one end of the piece of string to a door handle or chair.

2. Slide the straw onto the other end of the string.

3. Tie the free end of the string to something else in the room, such as another door handle or chair.

4. Blow up the balloon, and hold the end closed.

5. Use tape to fix the balloon to the straw, like this. Move the balloon and straw to one end of the string. Let go!

The balloon should zoom along the string. It's rocket science! The balloon lets out air, which pushes back against it, making it zoom forward.

You Can Be an Astronaut

Congratulations! You've been selected for the astronaut training program. Now the hard work starts! You'll have to go through all kinds of tests, exercises, and simulations. These prepare you for high-speed rocket travel and life in microgravity, as well as helping you cope in emergencies. The training includes ...

The Vomit Comet

To experience weightlessness, trainees fly in a plane that flies up and down in huge curves. As it zooms down, the passengers are in free fall and feel weightless.

It's nicknamed the Vomit Comet because it can cause terrible travel sickness!

Underwater Spacewalk

Astronauts train underwater wearing space suits. This enables them to float around freely as they do in space and learn how to breathe from the space suit's air supply.

Survival Skills

You'll also be taken to the middle of nowhere with a survival kit, to learn to survive in the wild if a spacecraft goes off-course.

Parachute Training

If something goes wrong on takeoff or landing, the astronauts may have to jump out, so parachute training is essential.

Activity: Train Like an Astronaut!

Your body needs to be as fit and strong as possible to go into space, so trainee astronauts do lots of fitness training. Try these real astronaut exercises!

Agility

- Put a row of obstacles on the floor, such as paper cups. Run along the row, in and out between the cups and back again. How many times can you do it?

Balance

- Stand on one leg while a friend throws a ball or beanbag for you to catch. You can hop to catch it, but keep the other leg off the ground.

Arm Strength

- Put one arm straight up and then the other. How long can you keep going?

Strength and Stamina

- Bear crawl: Crawl as far as you can on your hands and feet (not your knees).

- Crab walk: This is like the bear crawl but with your stomach upward, like this.

You Can Make Space Food

In space, you can't go to a superstore for some fresh milk or a banana! All the food that astronauts eat has to be carried or sent up from Earth. Astronauts also have to learn how to eat and drink in a special way.

Space food is often dried and stored in pouches. Astronauts add water to turn it into ready-to-eat food, such as soup, stew, or custard.

Some food is naturally long-lasting and easy to eat, like these nuts.

Astronauts have to drink from pouches or containers with straws, or the liquid would go everywhere! If food isn't too runny or crumbly, it can be eaten the normal way—like this breakfast wrap.

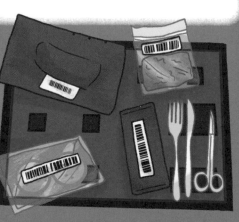

Did You Know?

- Delivery rockets bring regular food supplies. Astronauts can request foods they are missing from home.
- Fresh fruit is delivered to the ISS, but it must be eaten before it rots!
- It is possible to cook in space. Food is chopped inside a plastic bag and heated in a special oven (otherwise it wouldn't stay in a pan!)
- Salt and pepper come in liquid form. Tiny grains would float away and get lost, and could damage delicate space equipment.

Activity: Eat Like an Astronaut

Make your own space-style food, and eat it from the pouch! You could make several pouches and serve them to your family or friends.

You will need:

- A tablespoon
- Instant dessert mix
- A plastic food bag with a zip seal
- Dried milk powder
- A water bottle with a spout lid, filled with water
- A drinking straw

DEHYDRATED
SPACE DESSERT

STRAWBERRY
DELIGHT

1. Put several tablespoons of instant dessert mix into a food bag, along with one tablespoon of dried milk powder.

2. Seal the bag shut, leaving just one corner open. Carefully squirt some water into the bag through the hole, and seal it shut.

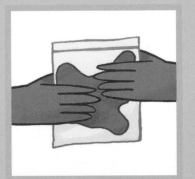

3. Squish and squeeze the bag to mix everything together. Add more water if necessary, to make a runny mixture.

4. Stick a straw into one corner of the bag, keeping the rest sealed. Try to slurp the dessert up using the straw.

To make it even more realistic, make space-style food labels to stick on the bags.

You Can Send a Message into Space

In 1977, NASA launched two space probes named Voyager 1 and Voyager 2. Their mission was to explore the outer Solar System. They carry on board a very special message from Earth.

Unusually, the mission does not have an end point. After passing the planets, the probes headed out of the Solar System and into interstellar space. Today, more than 40 years after launching, Voyager 1 has left the Solar System, and is the farthest human-made object from Earth. Long after we lose contact with them, both probes will continue their journey into space.

If there are intelligent aliens in the Universe, they might one day find a space probe, so scientists created a "Golden Record" for Voyager 1 and 2 to carry. It has recordings of sounds from Earth and messages from humans.

Each Golden Record has a cover, with a diagram showing the location of the Solar System and symbols showing how to play the record and decode the information. The record itself, called "The Sounds of Earth," is a disk with sounds recorded in a groove that spirals around it, like a traditional vinyl record. There's also a needle for playing the record.

The information on the record includes pictures from Earth stored in code; Earth sounds such as music, thunder, and animal noises; and greetings from Earth in 55 different languages.

Activity: What Would You Tell the Aliens?

If you could create a message to send into space, what would it say? If you were an alien, what would you want to know about planet Earth? In the space below, design your own Golden Record cover, and write down what sounds you would include on your record.

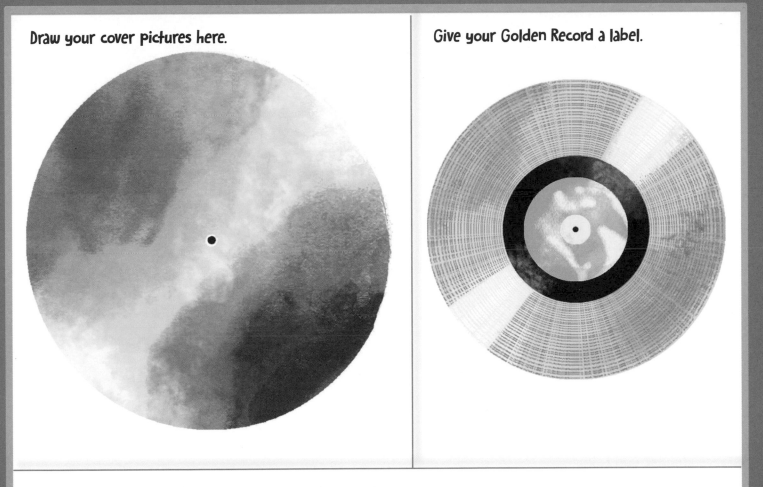

Draw your cover pictures here.

Give your Golden Record a label.

What sounds and pictures would you include?

You Can Sketch the Stars

Drawing a star by hand can quickly go wrong. But it's easy to do if you have the magic formula!

To start with, try this simple five-pointed star.

Draw five dots in a circle.	Start at one dot, and draw a line to the next-but-one dot around the edge.	Do the same again—miss the next dot, and draw a line to the second one.	And again ...	And again ...	And again.

You can draw many different stars like this, using one continuous line. All you need to do is:
- Draw a circle of dots—any number of dots.
- Choose a smaller number as the number of dots to count around the side.

There are just two rules:
1. The smaller number must be less than half the number of dots.
2. It must be a number that the first number can't be divided by.

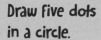

So for 12 dots, you can't have 1, 2, 3, or 4, but you can have 5.

Now start at one dot, count to the fifth dot around the edge, draw a line to that dot, and keep going until you're back to where you started, and you have a star!

Stars like this are called "star polygons." Each type has a name made up of its two numbers—so this is a "12/5" star polygon.

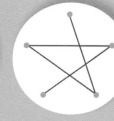

Activity: Star Circles

Here are some circles of dots for you to turn into stars. Follow the formula, and fill in the lines! Then try drawing your own on paper. What's the biggest star polygon you can create?

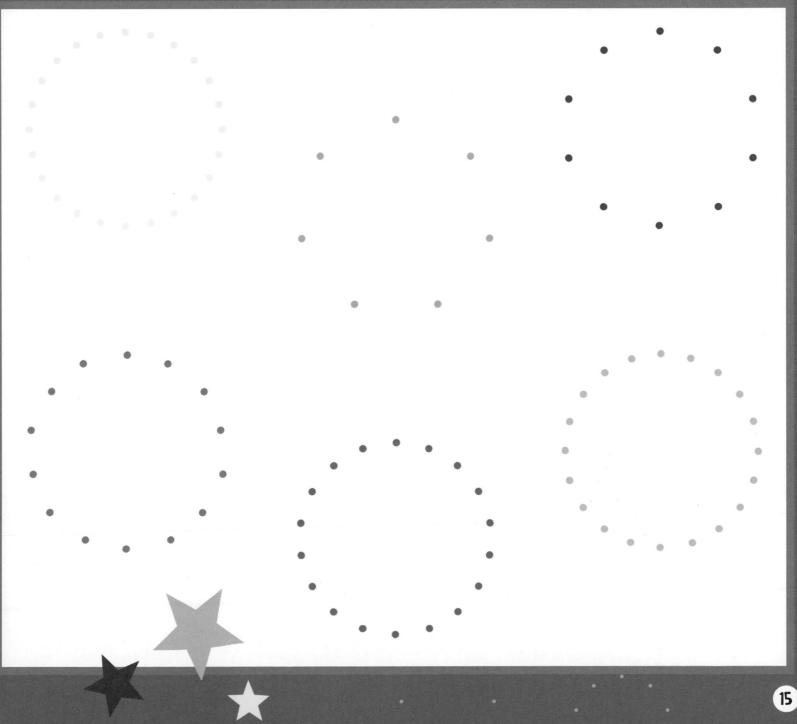

You Can Be a Code Breaker

Since ancient times, we've used numbers to encode things to keep them secret, and we still do today. When people shop online, their payment details are turned into number codes, so that they can be sent over the internet without being stolen.

One simple type of number code uses numbers to stand for letters. For example, you could match letters and numbers in a sequence, like this:

A B C D E F G H I J K L M N O P Q R S T U V W X Y Z
1 2 3 4 5 6 7 8 9 10 11 12 13 14 15 16 17 18 19 20 21 22 23 24 25 26

Can you decode it?

Then you could write a message using the code, like this:

20 8 1 20   23 1 19   5 1 19 25

parchment

The ancient Greeks could make coded messages using a special stick called a scytale. The sender would wrap a strip of parchment around the stick, then write the message along it. A messenger delivered the parchment on its own. Only someone with another scytale, the exact same diameter as the first one, could wind the strip around it and read the message.

HELP TRAPPED

Activity: Cipher Wheel

A cipher wheel lets you use different number codes for different messages—making them extra hard to crack. The sender and receiver of the code each need their own wheel.

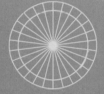

1. Draw two circles on the card, one 10cm (4 inches) across and one 8cm (3 inches) across. Cut them out, and make a hole through the middle of both with the pencil.

2. Draw straight lines across both circles, dividing them into 26 equal sections. (You could trace the picture below to make this easier.)

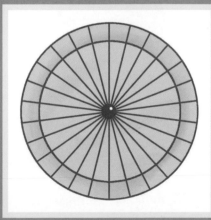

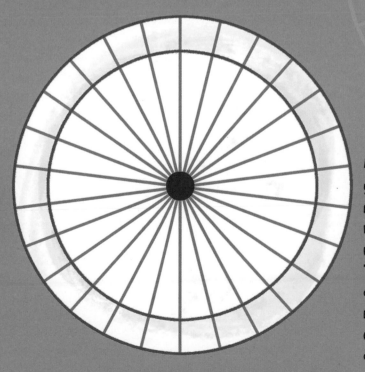

3. Write the 26 letters of the alphabet around the edge of the larger circle and the numbers 1–26 on the smaller circle. Pin the circles together with the pin or fastener.

4. Before you write your coded message, make a note of the number that lines up with the letter "A." This is your cipher code! Then write your message, replacing each letter with the corresponding number.

You Can Be a Cool Coder

Coders are amazing! Their work has transformed countless parts of our lives. Computer code helps us to stay in touch with friends, makes difficult tasks quick and easy, and puts information at our fingertips.

Thanks to coders, we can access knowledge and entertainment from almost anywhere.

Coding has made many professions easier, safer, and more creative.

Computers do all their calculations using patterns of 0s and 1s. This is called "binary code."

Some people think virtual reality is the future of coding. If you were a coder, what would you create?

Activity: Program a Robot

Here's a chance to program a robot (one of your friends) to obey your commands in order to stack some plastic cups. It sounds simple enough, but remember that the robot must follow each command exactly.

You will need:

- A friend (to become the "robot")
- 6 identical plastic cups
- A table

1. Ask one of your friends to become the robot.

2. Set the cups side by side on the table.

3. Explain that they have to do exactly what you say. They mustn't move at all if you don't tell them to!

4. You may give the robot four commands. None of them may be more than four words long.

5. Now try again—this time, with a stack of 6 cups! How many four-word commands do you need?

Commands

_____

_____

_____

_____

19

You Can Write Algorithms

Coders use the word "algorithm" to describe a set of rules to be followed in order to solve problems, or complete tasks. An experienced coder can devise clever algorithms to solve many different problems.

Factory robots' movements follow algorithms created by engineers, using code.

Before coders "go" to solve a problem, they "get set" with the right algorithm!

The word algorithm comes from "al-Khwarizmi," the name of a great Persian mathematician who lived 1,200 years ago.

If something goes wrong with a process, coders check whether the algorithm is correct.

Activity: Code Your Lunch

The rules in an algorithm must be in the right order! Sort the series of steps so that you can wind up with a tasty lunch—and not a horrible mess!

A. Remove from the toaster.

B. Press the cheese between the bread slices.

C. Toast the two slices.

D. Take out a piece of cheese. Remove wrapper.

E. Open refrigerator.

F. Spread butter on both slices.

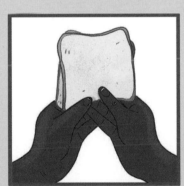

G. Choose two slices of bread.

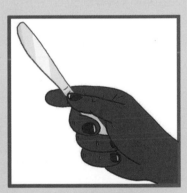

H. Get a butter knife.

1) _____

2) _____

3) _____

4) _____

5) _____

6) _____

7) _____

8) _____

You Can Learn Programming Languages

Coders use different languages, just as people speak different languages. The most popular programming languages include Python, Ruby, Java, JavaScript, and C++.

Just like a conversation, coders working together need to speak the same language.

Some computer languages are "all-purpose." Others are suited to special areas, such as composing music.

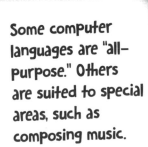

Coders give crazy names to their programming languages. Imagine learning Smalltalk, Malbolge, Shakespeare, or even one called "Ook!"

Most modern software concentrates on just four or five of the more than 250 computer languages.

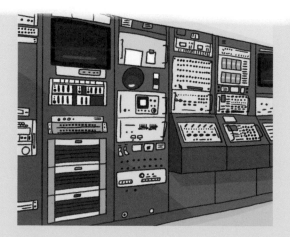

Activity: Capture the Candy

Here's a game for two or more players which uses computer language to move a counter toward a goal.

Each player will create a new "programming language" and invent a term in that language to mean "Go left," "Go right," "Repeat," "Go forward," and "Go backward." The aim of the game is to reach the candy using only the commands in your language.

You will need:

- 2 pieces of strong card
- Scissors
- Markers and paper
- 4 different coins
- A candy
- A chessboard

1. Cut the pieces of card into smaller playing cards. Give five to each player.

2. Each player must give their language a name, and draw a symbol on all five cards to represent it.

3. Each player writes an instruction on each card: "Go left," "Go right," "Repeat," "Go forward," and "Go backward."

4. Turn over all the cards. Working together, write a new word on each of them. The words must all be different.

5. Put the candy on one of the central squares of the board. Each player places their coin in a corner square.

6. Shuffle the cards and have each player take one. The word will tell them which "language" they need to use.

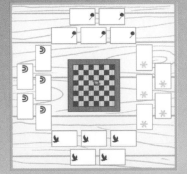

7. Give each player all the cards with a matching symbol. Now, they have one minute to memorize their "language."

8. Take away the cards! The players must write instructions in their language. Can they guide their coin to the candy?

You Can Build a Robotic Arm

To do useful jobs, robots need moving parts. A big part of robot engineering is designing and building arms, legs, claws, wheels, and other parts to make the robot work.

There are three basic methods for making a robot arm move:

Imagine you need your robot to have a moving arm. How do you make the movements happen?

1. With a motor system, the motor is a rotating part, usually powered by electricity.

2. A hydraulic system releases fluid into tubes to push and pull on moving parts.

3. In a cord or tendon system, strings or wires pull on the moving parts to control them.

A typical robot has multiple moving parts. Engineers have to work out how to make moving parts strong, but also small and light, so they don't get in the way of the movements or make the robot too heavy.

Activity: Moving Model

This simple robot arm demonstrates one type of arm joint and movement. If you can make this, you're on the way to building a robot!

You will need:

- Stiff card
- Scissors
- A split pin or noticeboard pin
- A drinking straw
- A wooden skewer
- Elastic bands

1. Cut out two pieces of stiff card, roughly the size and shape of a 15 cm (6 inch) ruler.

2. Pin the cardboard pieces together at one end with a split pin or noticeboard pin, to make a moving joint.

3. Attach a section of straw to one piece of cardboard, near the end, with an elastic band.

4. Push a wooden skewer through the straw and attach to the other section, near the joint, using an elastic band.

5. Push the skewer in and out to make the arm flex.

You Can Be a Robot Engineer

Most modern robots are computer-controlled. To tell a robot what to do, robot engineers write a computer program and download it into the robot's memory.

A program tells the robot how to move, react to different situations, and track its battery level.

You might program a waiter robot to find its way between tables and put food down when it gets to the right table.

Like any computer program, a robot's program is a list of instructions, written in a programming language such as C++, Python, or Java.

A pet dog robot is programmed to understand different speech commands and act on them.

Sit!
Fetch!
Beg!

Some industrial robots have their own control unit, called a teach pendant, for giving them instructions.

Activity: Which One Works?

These three robot engineers have built a brilliant new maze-exploring robot, but it's stuck in the middle of the maze. Each engineer has written a program to allow the robot to find its way out, but only one of these programs will work.

Casey's program:

1. Go forward.
2. If there is a wall in front of you, turn left.
3. Go back to line 1.

Takeo's program:

1. Go forward 3 blocks.
2. Turn right.
3. Go forward 1 block.
4. Turn left.
5. Go back to line 1.

Kavitha's program:

1. Go forward.
2. Whenever there's a gap to your right, turn right.
3. Whenever there's a wall in front of you and a wall to your right, turn left.

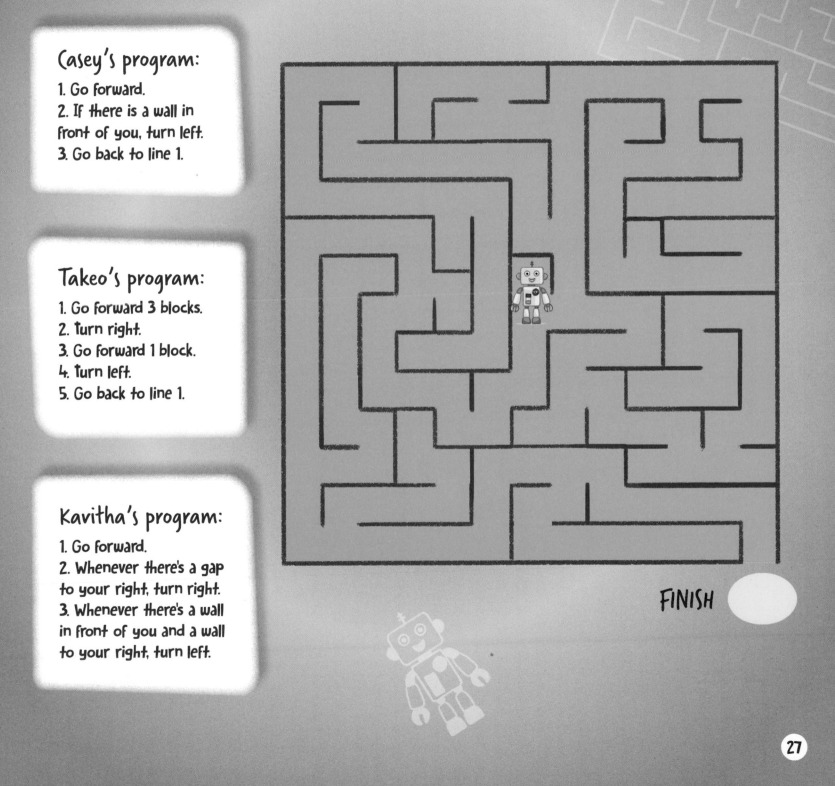

FINISH

You Can Design a Pet Robot

Would you prefer a real living pet, or a robot pet? Robot pets make great toys, but they also have other important uses. See if you can design one.

Robot pets have been around for a long time. They are usually dogs and cats, but there are others, too ...

Doctor Who had a robot dog, K9, in the 1970s.

Yume Neko is a cat robot from Japan.

Pleo is a robotic pet dinosaur.

This robot toy dog called AIBO was first launched in 1999.

Paro the seal is a robotic furry pet seal, designed to soothe and comfort people with memory loss.

Activity: Design a Robot Pet

You might love to have a robot pet cat, dog, or hamster, but what other animals might make good pets?

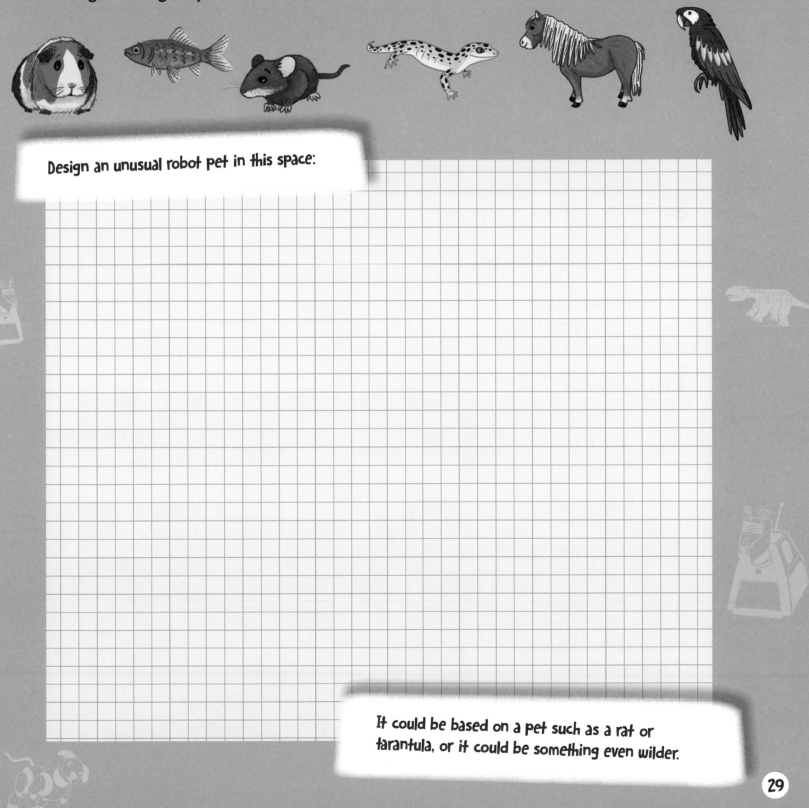

Design an unusual robot pet in this space:

It could be based on a pet such as a rat or tarantula, or it could be something even wilder.

You Can Design Gear Systems

Gears are wheels linked with cogs, which are the teeth around the edges of the wheel. Gears are used in machines to pass on movement and change its force, angle, speed, or direction.

Here's a simple gear system that changes the direction of rotation. The cogs of the gears interlock, so that when one wheel turns, it makes the other turn, too, but in the opposite direction.

This wheel turns clockwise ...

... making this wheel rotate the other way

Cogs

When a bigger gear turns a smaller gear, it changes the speed of rotation, making the smaller gear rotate faster.

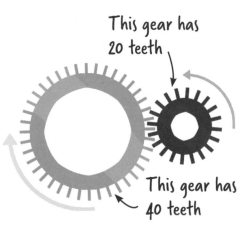

This gear has 20 teeth

This gear has 40 teeth

When the big gear rotates once, the smaller gear rotates twice, so it's twice as fast. It works the other way around too. A small gear driving a big gear makes the rotation slower.

This gear is upright

By putting gears at right angles to each other, you can also change the angle of rotation.

This gear is flat

Activity: Follow the Force

Some machines have many interconnecting gearwheels. Look at the machine on this page and see if you can figure out how it works.

If the boy turns the handle clockwise, as shown by the arrow, would the pointer at the end move up or down?

You Can Get Gliding

A glider is an unpowered plane. It has no engine—it just glides along on air currents until it finally lands. Paper gliders work in the same way and are fun to make!

For centuries, people have tried to fly by building bird wings and flapping them. It never worked, because humans aren't light or strong enough to fly by flapping.

875

Abbas ibn Firnas, an Islamic scientist living in Spain, may have been the first to make a glider flight at the age of 70, using wings made of silk on a wooden frame. He is said to have glided for several minutes.

1632

According to legend, Hezârfen Ahmed Çelebi built his own glider wings, to fly across the Bosphorus sea strait in Turkey, a distance of 1.5 km (about 1 mile).

1849

After testing numerous glider designs with no one onboard, British inventor George Cayley launched a glider from a hill carrying a 10-year-old boy! (He landed safely.)

1890s

German engineer Otto Lilienthal built and flew many gliders, making more than 2,000 flights.

Today

Today, people fly gliders as a hobby.

But birds also glide, with their wings spread out. When inventors began trying to fly by gliding instead of flapping, flight took off!

Activity: Paper Gliders

A paper plane is a type of simple glider.

Try making paper planes that glide as far as possible. You could have a contest with your friends.

Cut flaps into the wings and try folding them up or down.

1. First, make some basic paper planes. If you're not sure how, follow these diagrams.

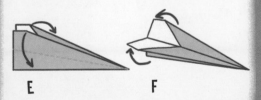

A

B

C

D

E

F

2. Try flying your planes. How far do they glide?

3. Use your inventing skills to improve the planes to make them fly farther. Here are some things you could do:

Fold the wing tips up.

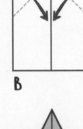

Attach tape to add weight to different parts of the plane.

Add an upright tail fin made of paper.

You could even invent a new type of paper plane!

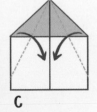

You Can Be a Pyrotechnician

According to ancient accounts, people in China began mixing chemicals to try to create potions that would allow them to live forever. They didn't succeed, but they did create something else—spectacular fireworks!

Around 1,200 years ago, Chinese experimenters found that certain chemical mixtures would explode when a flame touched them.

They realized that if they put the powder in a bamboo or paper tube, then set it on fire, it would shoot out and explode with a bang and a bright light.

Firework technology soon spread around the world. People began experimenting and mixing in other chemicals. Adding copper, for example, will make blue explosions.

Fireworks are still popular today at celebrations such as weddings, festivals, and New Year.

Activity: Cool Fireworks

One problem with fireworks is that being hot and explosive, they can be dangerous. So instead of making real fireworks, experiment with designing and making your own cool indoor fireworks display.

You will need:

- Paper
- Bendy straws
- Tape
- Scissors
- Tissue paper
- A balloon
- A toilet paper tube
- Sequins

To make straw rockets:

1. Wrap a small piece of paper around a bendy straw, and tape it in place to make a tube slightly wider than the straw.

2. Bend the end over, and tape it closed. Cut thin strips of tissue paper, and tape them to the closed end.

3. Fit the rocket over the long end of the bendy straw, and blow hard into the other end.

To make an exploding firework:

1. Tie the end of the balloon closed (without blowing it up), and cut off the top part.

2. Stretch the bottom end of the balloon over one end of the toilet paper tube, and tape it in place.

3. Put tiny pieces of tissue paper or sequins into the top of tube. Holding it firmly, pull the bottom of the balloon down, then let go.

You Can Be a Seismologist

Before a big earthquake, there are often smaller tremors or "foreshocks." These can be detected in advance by scientists called seismologists.

As long ago as 132 CE, Chinese scientist Zhang Heng invented an early seismoscope or quake detector. It was a large jar surrounded by model dragons with balls in their mouths. When the Earth shook, the dragons' mouths opened and dropped the balls.

Later seismoscopes used a heavy pendulum to detect shaking movements. This one, invented by Italian Andrea Bina in 1751, has a weight hanging on a string, with a pointer below it touching a tray of sand.

When the earth shakes, the pendulum moves and makes marks in the sand.

The wider the pattern of marks, the bigger the tremor.

This is a seismograph record of a huge earthquake that hit Japan in 2011.

In the 1800s, geologists developed seismographs—quake detectors that could draw a line on a moving piece of paper. They could now record tremors.

Activity: Model Seismoscope

Make your own model to see how a pendulum seismoscope works. You'll need a friend for this experiment—they will be your earthquake!

You will need:

- A paper cup
- Scissors
- A marker pen
- Coins, pebbles, or marbles
- String
- Tape
- A large cardboard box
- A long strip of paper
- A friend!

1. Make a hole in the bottom of the cup, and push the pen through so it points downward.

2. Half fill the cup with coins, pebbles, or marbles to make it heavier and hold the pen in place.

3. Cut a long piece of string, and tape the ends to the sides of the cup.

4. Stand the box on its side, and make a hole in the top. Thread the middle of the string through the hole.

5. Tape the string in place, so that the pen hangs just above the bottom of the box.

6. Cut two slots in the sides of the box at the same level as the pen tip. Feed a long strip of paper through, so that the pen touches it.

Ask your friend to gently shake the table while you pull the paper through the box.

You Can Be an Architect

There are many different types of architect. In a large architecture company, there may be various roles, such as designing outdoor areas or making technical drawings.

Meet the team!
If drawing is your thing, you'd make a great design architect. They focus on designing how a building will look, and create the first sketches on paper.

A production architect mainly works on a computer, making detailed, technical drawings that show exactly how to construct the building. Great for computer-lovers with brilliant attention to detail!

Some architects spend time visiting building sites and managing the build. On-site architects check that the builders are following the plans properly, and that they have what they need.

Or you could be a landscape architect, focusing on outside spaces. You might design the garden, courtyard, or roof terrace of a building your company is working on.

Activity: This Needs Fixing!

Betty the builder and her team are hard at work building a new house, but there are several problems. Can you match each problem to the architect who can fix it?

Who should I call?

1. The front door that's been ordered is too big for the gap! Someone needs to check the technical drawings.

2. The people next door would like some extra trees planted between the houses for privacy.

3. The client wants to see a sketch of how the house would look with bigger windows.

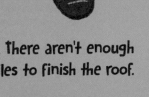

4. There aren't enough tiles to finish the roof.

Frank
Design architect

Kazuyo
Production architect

Louis
On-site architect

Julia
Landscape architect

You Can Be a Structural Engineer

However beautiful your buildings might be, the most important thing is that they don't fall over! Architects and structural engineers use these rules to make sure buildings are strong enough to stay standing up.

Strong walls

If you've ever built something out of plastic bricks, you'll know that overlapping them makes the walls strong. Brick and stone walls work like this, too.

Holding together

The parts of a building all have to be linked together to make it strong. The beams in a roof, for example, hold the sides of the roof together so it doesn't fall flat.

Good foundations

Buildings must be firmly fixed into the ground, and stand on a solid base, called a foundation. It's often made of concrete.

The power of triangles

Triangles are very strong shapes, as they don't bend or collapse under pressure. So using triangle or diagonal shapes makes buildings stronger.

The Eiffel Tower in Paris is made of iron in a lattice of triangles, making it very strong. It was only meant to be temporary, built to commemorate 100 years since the French Revolution in 1889, but has been standing ever since!

The whole tower has a triangle-like shape, too. It's widest at the bottom, so it's extremely stable.

Activity: Spaghetti Tower

Find out how to build strong structures by experimenting with spaghetti and marshmallows.

You will need:

- Dried spaghetti
- Marshmallows

Take some pieces of spaghetti and use the marshmallows to fix them together to make a structure.

Here are four ideas to get you started:

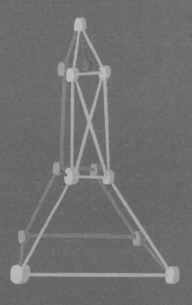

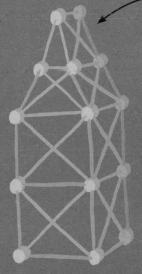

If you don't have spaghetti and marshmallows, you can use thin sticks and model clay.

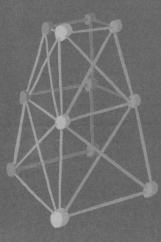

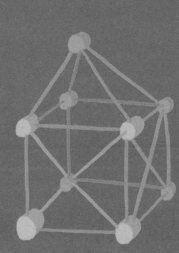

What's the tallest tower you can make that doesn't fall down?

You Can Be a Civil Engineer

They're not quite the same as buildings, but architects and civil engineers have also designed amazing bridges.

There are several types of bridges, with different ways of getting across a gap.

A beam bridge is one of the simplest designs. A flat road or walkway rests on a row of pillars.

An arch bridge uses the ancient stone arch system to stay up.

A truss bridge has a grid of iron or steel girders, often arranged in triangle patterns, to give it strength.

A suspension bridge has towers with cables strung between them. The walkway or road hangs from the cables.

The best bridges are safe, strong, AND beautiful, too!

Activity: Bridge Challenge

Your challenge: to build a model bridge across a gap using just paper, string, and tape. It has to be strong enough to hold up a heavy weight.

You will need:
- Books
- Sheets of paper
- Tape
- Lots of string
- An unopened drinks can or food tin

1. Make two piles of books, each about the same height. Position them about 50 cm (20 inches) apart—this is the gap your bridge will cross.

Rolling paper into a tube is a good way to make it stronger.

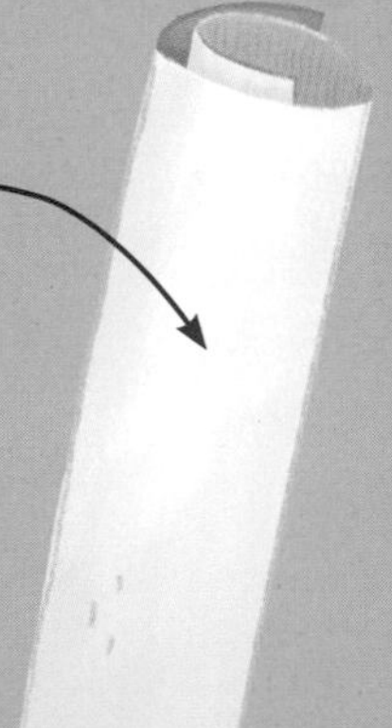

2. Get designing! Decide how your bridge will work and build it using just paper, tape, and string.

Remember, triangles are good shapes for strong structures, too.

3. To test it, try standing the can or tin in the middle!

You Can Be an Eco-Architect

As we all know, it's good to use less energy and make things from sustainable resources. Buildings can help us to do this!

Sustainability means using natural materials in such a way that they won't run out in the future.

Eco-buildings are designed to be sustainable and to use less energy, both while they're being built, and when they're being used. Architects can also include features that save water, and provide a habitat for wildlife.

Heat exchanger ventilates the house without letting cold air in

Solar panels use sunlight to make electricity

Green plant-covered roof holds in heat and provides a wildlife habitat

Roof collects rainwater to water plants and flush toilets

Eco-shower reuses water

Large window facing the Sun helps the house warm up inside

Wood and bamboo are renewable and use less energy than concrete walls and PVC window frames

Triple-glazed windows and thick wall insulation keep heat in, reducing the need for a fireplace or stove

Line for drying clothes in the Sun

Electric car charging point

Outdoor area with lots of trees and plants helps wildlife

Bike store

Activity: Do You Know Your Eco-Enemies?

You're designing a new housing estate and you want to make the homes as eco-friendly as possible.

Here are some features you could include. However, three of them are well-known for not being good for the environment. See if you can identify them.

Circle three things that you don't think should be included in your eco-homes.

Window boxes

Solar panels

Clothes line

Bike shed

Coal-burning stove

Clothes dryer

Water collector

Paved-over outdoor space

Rooftop wind turbine

You Can Be a Fingerprint Expert

The skin on your fingertips is covered in patterns of tiny ridges. When you touch shiny surfaces, your sweat leaves a mark in the shape of these fingertip patterns, called fingerprints. Forensic scientists can see these prints more clearly by dusting them with powder.

Each person has a slightly different set of patterns. If there are fingerprints at a crime scene, you might be able to identify who made them!

Although your fingerprints are unique, the same types of shapes show up in everyone's prints. They're called arches, loops, and whorls.

Arch

Loop

Double loop

Mixed figure

Whorl

Activity: Take Your Prints

When police officers arrest a suspect, they often make a record of their fingerprints using ink and paper. Try recording your own fingerprints! Can you see any arches, loops, or whorls?

You will need:

- A blunt pencil
- Two pieces of white paper
- Tape
- Scissors

1. Use a pencil to scribble on one piece of white paper, going over the same area again and again.

2. Rub a clean, dry fingertip over the patch of pencil.

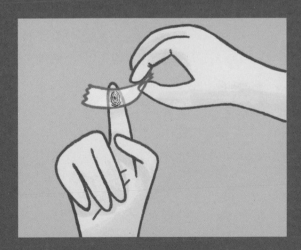

3. Stick a piece of tape over the fingertip, then pull gently away. Now you have a record of your print.

4. Stick the tape onto a clean piece of paper and label it. Repeat steps 1–4 with your other fingers —or with friends and family.

You Can Be a Forensic Scientist

When forensic scientists have collected material containing DNA, they take it to a lab. First, they extract, or take out, the DNA from its cell. Then they study the DNA to see if it matches up with DNA taken from suspects.

Studying someone's DNA cannot tell us exactly how they look or behave, because human beings are very complex. But here are five things that DNA can tell us about an unknown suspect ...

1. If they are likely to have light (e.g. blue or green), dark (brown or black), or hazel eyes.

2. If they are likely to have red hair.

3. If they are the same person as, or in the same family as, someone who has already given a DNA sample.

4. If they are male or female.

5. If they have a high risk of suffering from certain diseases that are passed through a family's DNA.

Activity: Extract DNA From a Strawberry

Strawberry cells contain lots of DNA molecules—much more than human cells—so they are quite easy to extract and see. A single molecule of DNA is too thin to see with the naked eye, but this experiment makes the strands of strawberry DNA clump together so we can take a look.

You will need:

 You will need an adult to pour and measure the rubbing alcohol!

- A strawberry
- A zip-seal freezer bag
- A measuring container
- 90 ml (6 tablespoons) water
- A measuring spoon
- 10 ml (2 teaspoons) dishwashing liquid
- ¼ teaspoon salt
- A strainer/sieve
- A bowl
- A tall drinking glass
- 15 ml (1 tablespoon) rubbing alcohol or surgical spirits, chilled
- Tweezers

1. Put the strawberry in a freezer bag, then pour in the water, dishwashing liquid, and salt. Remove as much air from the bag as possible, then seal it.

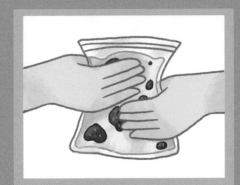

2. Press the bag with your fingers for at least 2 minutes to thoroughly mash up the strawberry. The soap and salt break down the fruit's cells, so that they release their DNA.

3. Press the mash through a strainer into a bowl. Then pour it from the bowl into a tall glass.

4. Ask an adult to gently drip 1 tablespoon of chilled rubbing alcohol or surgical spirits onto the surface of the strawberry liquid.

5. You will see a layer of white, stringy goop near the top of the mixture—this is strawberry DNA! Use tweezers to pull out the DNA, and take a good look at it!

You Can Be a Dental Detective

Everyone has a unique set of teeth. Teeth are different sizes and shapes. Your dentist has a record of your teeth, because they keep the X-rays that they take when checking for cavities. If someone lost their memory, it might be possible to identify them using their dental records.

Children have 20 teeth by about the age of 3. Adults have up to 32 teeth, the final "wisdom" teeth growing in at 17–21 years old. In adults, teeth wear down from a lifetime of chewing.

Canines, which are used for ripping food, are more pointed.

Incisors help you bite off food.

Molars, which are flatter, are for grinding up food.

"Wisdom" teeth are the final molars to emerge.

Activity: Chocolate Bites!

Since everyone's teeth are slightly different, everyone leaves a different bite mark. When a thief broke into Cherry's Chocolate Shop, they made a silly mistake—they bit into a bar of chocolate and then left it behind, giving us a record of their bite. Which suspect bit the chocolate?

The suspects:

Suspect 1

Suspect 2

Suspect 3

Suspect 4

You Can Be a Handwriting Expert

Strange as it seems, some criminals may write a letter to a newspaper or the police. Handwriting experts try to match the handwriting to samples of writing from suspects. Experts might also be called in when someone is suspected of forging someone else's signature on a document.

Look at loops and curls on g, y, f, and j.

The quick brown fox jumps over the lazy dog.
The quick brown fox jumps over the lazy dog.
The quick brown fox jumps over the lazy dog.
The quick brown fox jumps over the lazy dog.
The quick brown fox jumps over the lazy dog.

Are all the letters connected to each other or separate?

Are upstrokes vertical or slanted?

Handwriting experts look at these key points:

1. The ways the letters are formed—everyone writes each letter a little differently.

2. The style of writing—the way handwriting is taught has changed over the years and differs from region to region.

3. The smoothness and darkness of the lines show how hard the writer presses and how fast they write.

4. Signs that the writer is disguising their handwriting. Shaky starts and lots of pen lifts reveal they are writing slowly and possibly copying.

Activity: Match the Handwriting!

A bicycle thief left a rude note for the bike's owner. Handwriting samples have been supplied by three suspects. Who wrote the note?

Note Left at the Crime Scene:

I stole your bike! Ha ha!

Handwriting Samples from Suspects:

Suspect A   I stole your bike!

Suspect B   I stole your bike!

Suspect C   I stole your bike!

No two samples of handwriting from one person will be completely identical! Look for similarities between samples, but also watch out for differences that could rule out any suspects.

You Can Be a Lie Detector

In some countries, "lie detector" machines were once used. They tested for signs of nervousness, such as a fast heartbeat. Unfortunately, innocent people can get nervous, and guilty people who are used to telling lies can pass them, so they are no longer used by the police.

When we feel nervous or afraid, the brain releases hormones that give us a burst of energy, so we can run away from or fight the danger. Here are some signs that those hormones have been released:

1. Faster heartbeat
2. Faster breathing
3. Quicker blinking
4. Blushing and sweating
5. Pursed lips because of a dry mouth

Never believe that a suspect is guilty until you have collected and tested evidence—and, most importantly, before they have received a trial in a court of law.

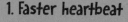

Activity: Take Your Pulse!

Your heart is a muscle that pumps blood around your body by squeezing. Every time the heart squeezes, it sends a wave, or pulse, of blood through your veins. You can feel this pulse most easily where a vein passes over a bone, such as at your wrist. Try this experiment to see the effect of exercise on your pulse.

1. To find the pulse on your wrist, place two fingers at the base of your thumb, then slide your fingers straight down onto your wrist. Press gently until you feel a faint, throbbing pulse.

2. Ask your partner to start the stopwatch. Count how many times you feel your pulse in 1 minute. Your partner should say "Stop" when the minute is up, then write down the number.

3. Now run on the spot for 1 minute.

4. As soon as you stop running, ask your partner to start the stopwatch. Count how many times you feel your pulse in 1 minute.

5. Compare the two heart rates. What do you notice?

You Can Be a Doctor

What would we do without doctors? You need a doctor if you have asthma, break your arm, or catch a nasty virus. And those are just a few of the thousands of illnesses, injuries, and other problems that doctors have to deal with.

The human body is amazing, but complicated! It can go wrong in a LOT of different ways. So doctors have to learn a lot about all the parts of the body, and how to fix all kinds of problems. By spotting a particular disease, finding the right medicine, or knowing what to do in an emergency, doctors often save lives.

When people feel sick, they usually visit a family doctor. But there are many other types of doctor you could be:

A family doctor sees people who don't feel well, and prescribes medicine.

A hospital doctor works in a hospital, where patients go if they have a more serious problem.

A surgeon carries out operations, or surgery.

A flying doctor travels in a plane or helicopter to emergencies in remote or hard-to-reach places.

Activity: Body Part Spotter

To start with, let's get to know the basics of the human body!

Follow the lines to match the body parts to their correct names.

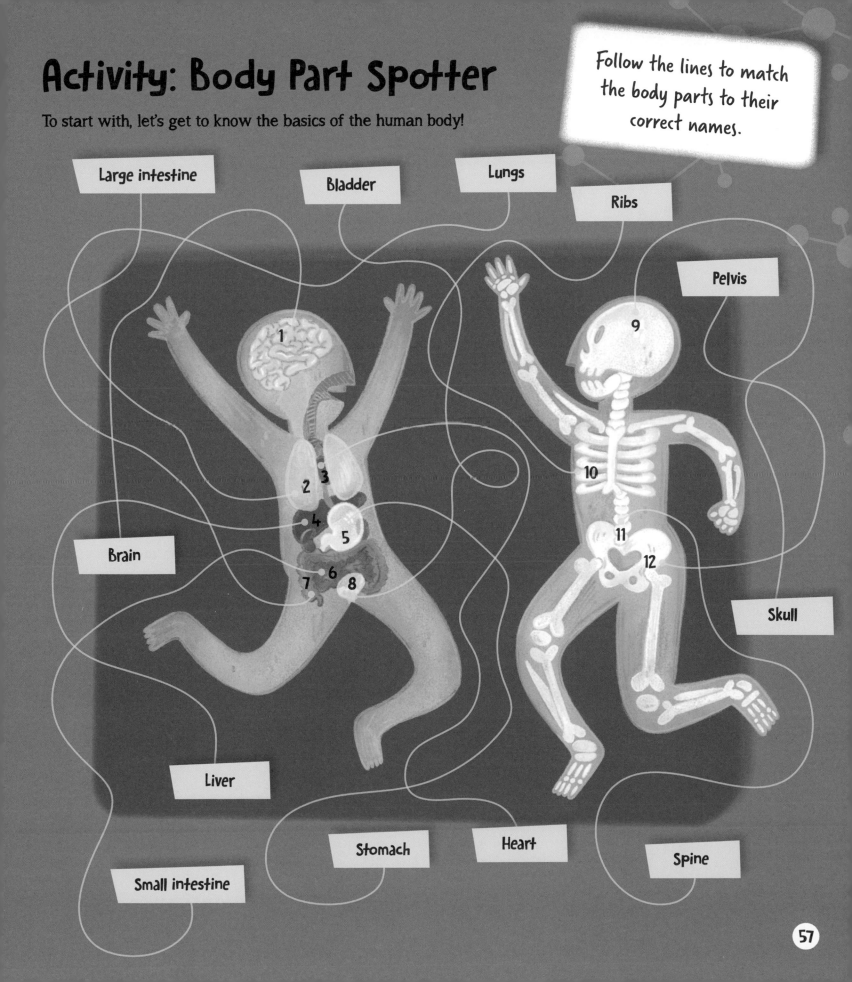

Large intestine

Bladder

Lungs

Ribs

Pelvis

Brain

Liver

Skull

Small intestine

Stomach

Heart

Spine

You Can Be a Podiatrist

Feet have a tough life. They get stood on all day, they kick balls and climb walls, and they get squished into tight shoes. Podiatrists are foot doctors who can help.

Of course, we need shoes to protect our feet, but they can cause problems, too.

Have you been looking after these feet?

Too-narrow shoes can cause an ingrown toenail. This is when the sides of the nail dig into the skin of the toe.

Ingrown toenail

High-heeled shoes can cause bunions, which are bumps on the toe joints, and hammer toes, when toes curl over instead of lying straight.

Comfy sneakers are good for your feet, but they can get sweaty!

Flat shoes don't support the foot very well, and can make your feet ache.

New shoes or sandals can rub and cause foot blisters.

Feet can also get fungal infections, like athlete's foot and nail fungus. These are actually fungi, and are related to mushrooms!

Verrucas are a type of wart that grow on the soles of the feet. The virus that causes them often hangs around in changing rooms and swimming pools.

Why are some feet so stinky? Feet sweat a lot, partly because they're inside hot shoes. If they're not washed often enough, the sweat gets old and starts to smell bad!

Activity: A Pair of Problem Feet

Mr. Steptoe has NOT been looking after his feet. They're in a terrible state, so he's come to see you. Can you circle six problems with his feet?

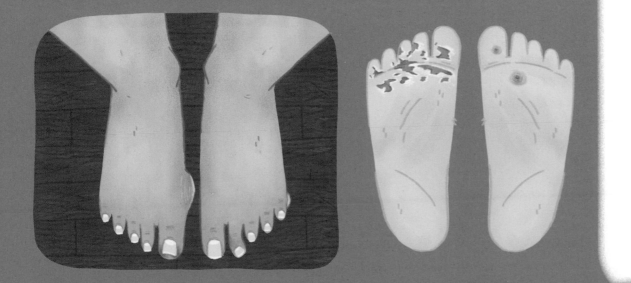

These are the foot conditions to look out for:

Ingrown toenail

Hammer toe

Bunion

Blister

Verruca

Athlete's foot

You Can Be an Orthopedic Surgeon

Bones are strong, but sometimes they break. Luckily, just like skin, they can also rebuild themselves! Orthopedic surgeons are bone specialists who can help them to heal by making sure the broken bones are kept still.

Arm and leg bones are among the most common breaks, or fractures. That's probably because these bones are quite long and thin.

Help!

If a doctor thinks a bone might be broken, they will use an X-ray to look at it. The X-ray above shows a break in the radius, a bone in the lower arm.

An X-ray is a type of photo that uses X-rays instead of normal light. X-rays can shine through the body and take a picture of the bones inside.

To make sure the bone will heal and repair itself, it needs to be held in the right position. So the normal treatment for a bone fracture is a splint or cast. It holds the broken bone still until it's back to normal.

Plaster cast

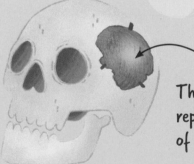

This skull plate replaces a section of broken skull.

Some broken bones are hard to put a cast on—like a skull, or a bone that is broken in several places. For these fractures, doctors do operations to repair or replace the broken bone, using metal pins or plates.

Activity: Dr. X. Ray

Dr. Xanna Ray works in the emergency room, and she has a lot of patients with broken bones today. Look at all these X-ray photos!

Help the doctor spot the fracture on each X-ray photo. Can you also work out which parts of the body they belong to?

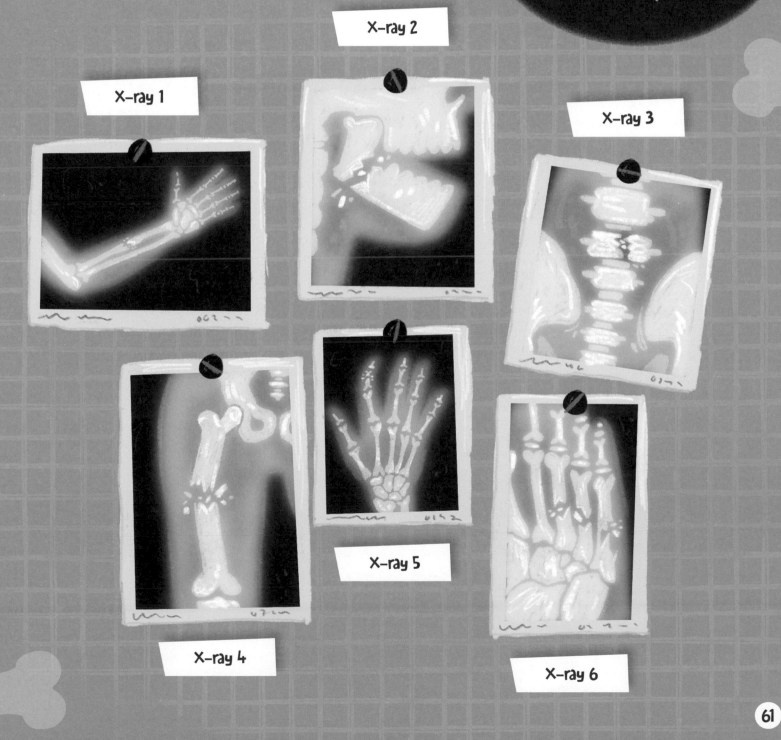

X-ray 1

X-ray 2

X-ray 3

X-ray 4

X-ray 5

X-ray 6

You Can Be a Vet

If you have a pet, you probably take it to a pet vet. They usually have a surgery in a town or city, where they see lots of pets.

Cluck cluck!

But that's just one type of vet. There are vets who work with other animals, too—farm animals, zoo animals, working animals, and sometimes even wild animals.

Pet vet

A pet cat goes to a pet vet!

Farm vet

A farm vet visits farms to treat animals such as cows, horses, sheep, pigs, and chickens. Or they might work with more unusual farm animals, like ostriches or alpacas.

Zoo vet

Some vets work in zoos, looking after anything from tree frogs and parrots to pandas, tigers, and elephants.

Wildlife vet

Wild animals sometimes need vets, too. Wildlife vets might work at a wildlife reserve, or care for wild animals that have been injured.

Activity: Which Vet?

These unfortunate animals are all feeling under the weather in one way or another, and they all need help. Can you send each animal to the right type of vet?

Draw lines to match the animals to the correct vets.

1. A wild orca that's getting too thin

2. A guinea pig with a cough

3. A baby gorilla with a broken leg

4. A llama with a sore eye

DR. BARKING Pet vet

DR. MUDDI Farm vet

DR. LYONS Zoo vet

DR. WILD Wildlife vet

You Can Be an Animal Surgeon

Sometimes, an animal needs an operation, also called surgery. It could be to mend a damaged organ, remove a swallowed object, or take out a body part that's sick or not working.

Operations on animals are similar to operations on humans, although the patient may be much bigger or smaller!

This orangutan has appendicitis, and has to have its appendix removed.

The operation happens in an operating room. It has to be very clean to make sure germs don't get into the animal's body.

An anesthetist gives the animal medicine to make it fall asleep and not feel pain.

Vet nurses and technicians look after the equipment and pass tools to the surgeon.

The surgeon operates, then sews up the opening neatly.

Losing a leg

Sometimes, an accident or illness means an animal has to have a body part, such as a tail or leg, cut off, or amputated.

If an animal has lost two legs, it can sometimes have a kind of animal wheelchair made for it.

Activity: The Operating Room

Dr. Barking is carrying out an operation on Woofer, a pet dog. Here's a bird's-eye view of the operating room. Can you identify all the people and things in the picture?

Draw lines and arrows to match everything up!

Dr. Barking, the surgeon

Anesthetist

Vet nurses

Woofer, the patient

Surgical tool trolley

Monitoring screen

Operating table

You Can Be a Pet Psychologist

Can animals be good or bad? Not really! They just follow their natural instincts, and don't mean to be "naughty."

Some vets, called pet psychologists, specialize in how animals behave. They might visit the animal at home and try to find out what's causing the problem.

Vets can help owners to train their pets, or change the way they behave.

When a cat scratches furniture, it might be trying to release scent from its paws to mark its territory. There are special sprays owners can use to help. Some sprays smell bad to cats and keep them away. Others contain chemicals that calm the cat down.

Sometimes people bring their pets to the vet because they act in a way that's hard to handle—for example, dogs might bite, bark, jump up on people, or run away.

Dogs are especially good at learning. The best way to train a dog is to reward them when they behave well.

Clicker

Snacks

The reward can be a snack, but too many snacks isn't good! So a clicker can be used instead. It makes a sound that's linked to a reward. Soon, the sound itself becomes a reward, and makes the dog happy.

Punishing a dog for doing something wrong is mean and doesn't work! Instead, the dog gets a reward when it gets it right.

Activity: Dogs in the Park

One reason we train dogs to behave well is so that they don't bother or harm other animals or people. Some of the dogs in Pettifer Park are behaving perfectly. But a few are not! Can you find six dogs behaving badly?

Circle the dogs that you think could benefit from some training.

You Can Be a Vet Scientist

Veterinary scientists, or vet scientists, are experts on animal health. Instead of actually dealing with animals all day, they mostly work in labs, doing a range of different jobs.

It's the perfect job if you love science and mathematics as well as animals!

Studying

This involves finding out more about animal health, and which treatments work best for different animal illnesses.

Testing

When a vet takes a blood sample or scan to test for a disease, it goes off to the lab, where scientists look at it to see what's wrong.

Teaching

Vet scientists often teach students, too, training them to be the next generation of vets.

Inventing

Some vet scientists work on new ideas and inventions. These could be new medicines, types of bandages, or prosthetic limbs. Or they might create things that help student vets learn, such as artificial horse skin. This brilliant invention lets student vets have a go at stitching up a wound, without having to use a real horse.

Artificial horse skin

Activity: Under the Microscope

Are you good at spotting things? As a vet scientist, you might have to look at an image and check for anything unusual. The pictures below show a dog's blood cells seen through a microscope. The dog has an illness that makes some of its blood cells clump together in little clusters.

the normal cells look like this ...

And the clusters look like this ...

this is what your dog patient's cells look like ...

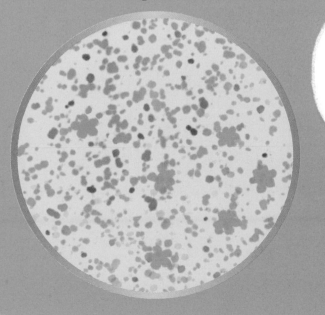

There are six clusters in among the normal blood cells. Can you find them all?

You Can Be a Paleontologist

Being a paleontologist is an exciting, fascinating job—but it's hard work, too! It involves doing a wide range of very different tasks, and working in different places.

These are all the different types of things a typical dinosaur paleontologist might get up to in their job.

Working at dig sites, excavating fossils.

Studying and piecing together fossils in the lab.

Making computer models and scans of fossils.

You'd never be bored!

Writing papers or books about fossil discoveries.

Teaching classes on paleontology.

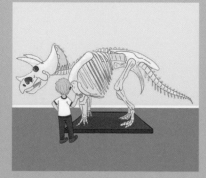
Working in a museum, preparing fossils for display.

Activity: Are You a Natural?

Do you have the skills, abilities, and personality to make a great paleontologist? Try this quiz to find out.

1. What's your best subject at school?
a) Science
b) Art
c) Dance

2. What's your bedroom like?
a) A bit messy
b) Tidy and organized
c) A total pigsty!

3. What's your ideal holiday accommodation?
a) A ski chalet
b) A luxury hotel with a pool
c) A tent

4. Do you prefer hanging out ...
a) With lots of friends
b) On your own with a good book
c) A bit of both!

5. Which of these hobbies appeals to you most?
a) Horse-riding
b) Model-making
c) Playing in a band

6. You're meeting a friend, but they're late. What do you do?
a) Wait at least half an hour
b) Wait a few minutes
c) Go home straight away

You Can Be a Dinosaur Detective

By looking at rock layers, paleontologists have figured out when dinosaurs were alive, and how long for.

Dinosaurs existed for over 180 million years—that's over 50 times longer than humans!

The history of the Earth is divided into large sections of time known as eras.

Era	Time (millions of years ago)	Life on Earth
Present day	0	
Cenozoic era		
	66.4	
Mesozoic era		
	245	
Paleozoic era		
	540	
Proterozoic era		

Each era is divided into shorter periods. The Mesozoic era, or dinosaur age, has three periods:

Cretaceous period	145–66 million years ago	
Jurassic period	200–145 million years ago	
Triassic period	251–200 million years ago	

Activity: Dino Dates

Which of these dinosaurs lived at the same time, and which lived in completely different periods and could never have existed alongside each other?

Use the Mesozoic timeline to find out when these dinosaurs existed. Then draw lines connecting the dinosaurs that were alive during the same period as each other, and sort them into pairs or groups.

9

Plateosaurus

1.

Saltopus

8

Triceratops

2

Allosaurus

7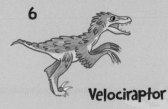

Stegosaurus

3

Brachiosaurus

6

Velociraptor

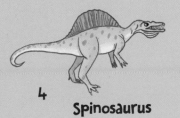

5

4

Spinosaurus

Iguanodon

You Can Be a Weather Scientist

Working with the weather involves a whole range of different skills. Whatever you're good at or like doing, it could be useful!

Weather scientists do a lot of measuring, checking, and recording facts and figures. They need good attention to detail—great for those who love mathematics!

This is fantastic!

I'm cold and I want to go home.

For checking conditions in the wild, you need to love the outdoors—whatever the weather!

Big, powerful computers are used to calculate weather forecasts, so programming and other computer skills could come in handy.

Good morning, and welcome to the weather show!

Computer art and design skills are important for turning weather data into maps and graphs that people can easily understand.

For presenting weather forecasts, you need to be friendly, chatty, and good at speaking clearly and keeping your cool!

Activity: temperature Map

The weather computer has used a set of temperature measurements to make this map for a television weather report. Each band across the map shows a different temperature range, with figures ranging from a frosty 0 °C (32 °F) up to a toasty 30 °C (86 °F).

Your job is to look at the key below and complete the map, making it easy for viewers to understand at a glance.

Use your pens or pencils to show the temperatures on the weather map.

16 °C   0 °C   12 °C   9 °C   6 °C   13 °C   17 °C   18 °C   23 °C   30 °C   25 °C   24 °C   18 °C   20 °C   19 °C   18 °C   11 °C   14 °C

0–5 °C   **6–10 °C**   **11–15 °C**   **16–20 °C**   **21–25 °C**   **26–30 °C**

You Can Be a Weather Forecaster

When you watch a forecast on TV, or check the weather on your computer or phone, you're looking at the results of a vast amount of weather science!

To make a weather forecast, weather scientists have to collect a huge amount of data. It comes from weather stations, weather ships, weather balloons, and weather satellites in space.

All this data is fed into powerful supercomputers. They use the existing movements of air, water, and heat in the atmosphere to predict what will probably happen next.

The data includes temperatures, cloud patterns, wind speeds, and lots of other measurements, along with previous weather patterns, such as the average temperature for the time of year, and the direction in which storms usually travel.

Your location

Now

14 °C
57 °F

5%

Sunny spells

UV Low

The data is processed and turned into weather maps to show on TV, or information that can be used in apps, radio reports, or newspapers.

And now for the weather!

Activity: Write the Script!

When weather forecasters present a TV forecast, they don't just read out a list of temperatures and other facts. They use chatty, everyday language instead, to make it friendly and easy to understand.

Can you turn the weather data below into a friendly weather forecast?

Write a script for your forecast in the space below.

WEATHER DATA / MAY 2ND

9 am	1 pm	6 pm
Temperature: 16 °C (61 °F)	Temperature: 19 °C (66 °F)	Temperature: 24 °C (75 °F)
Wind speed: 10 km/h (6 mph)	Wind speed: 8 km/h (5 mph)	Wind speed: 5 km/h (3 mph)
Chance of rainfall: 21%	Chance of rainfall: 11%	Chance of rainfall: 4%

WEATHER FORECASTER'S SCRIPT

It'll start off a little chilly, but don't worry, things will soon warm up!

You Can Predict Extreme Weather

Wild, extreme weather such as storms, blizzards, and burning heat can be bad news and lead to disasters. Predicting these events gives people a chance to prepare.

Tornadoes flatten homes and fill the air with dangerous, whirling debris.

A drought, meaning a long time without rain, can stop crops from growing, causing food shortages and famines.

Ice storms and heavy snow can cut off roads, leaving people stranded.

Weather forecasts play an important part in keeping people safe.

Heatwaves dry out the land and can lead to wildfires.

Tropical cyclones can bring destructive winds as well as flooding from heavy rain.

When heavy rain soaks the soil on a hillside, it can suddenly slip down in a landslide.

Heavy snow on mountains can result in hazardous avalanches.

Activity: Safe House

One way to protect against a weather disaster is to build a home that can survive a nasty storm, instead of getting blown or washed away. Can you design a hurricane-proof house that won't be damaged by wind or floods?

Draw your design in the space below.

What shape do you think might help wind flow past without breaking bits off?

How could you keep a house safe from floodwater?

You Can Harness Wind Power

Meteorologists (weather scientists) measure wind speed to help predict the weather. Wind power can be destructive, but it can also be used to make energy. Wind power, like solar power, is a renewable resource. Unlike oil or gas, it will never run out.

The powerful winds of a hurricane can damage houses, flip cars, and uproot trees. Accurate weather predictions can warn communities about dangerous storms, such as hurricanes.

Scientists use special instruments called anemometers to measure wind speed. One of the best ways of predicting the weather is to judge whether that speed is increasing or decreasing.

Meteorologists use the Beaufort Scale to describe wind speeds. The scale begins with "0" (no wind) and goes up to "12" (hurricane force).

Environmentalists can tap wind power. The force of the wind makes the blades of wind turbines spin. That spinning, in turn, causes machinery to turn inside, providing the power to generate (produce) electricity.

Activity: Wind Power

Create a homemade anemometer. Test it outside to catch the breeze. It should spin faster when the wind picks up.

You will need:

- A hole punch
- 5 small paper cups
- 2 drinking straws
- 1 pencil with eraser
- A poster pin

1. Assemble everything you need on a table or counter.

2. Punch four holes in one of the cups—opposite each other and just below the rim.

3. Push the two straws through the holes so that they form an "X."

4. Punch two holes, midway down and 3cm (1 inch) apart, in each of the other four cups.

5. Thread a straw through the holes in each cup. Make sure the cups face the same way.

6. Poke a hole in the base of the middle cup, then push your pencil through the hole, eraser end first.

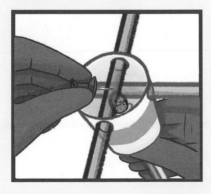

7. Carefully press the poster pin down through the straw junction and into the eraser, which should be sitting just underneath. Now your anemometer is ready!

You Can Be an Environmental Scientist

Environmental scientists monitor the causes of global warming. They know that gases released into the atmosphere form a blanket around Earth, trapping heat in our atmosphere.

Scientists warn us to eat less beef because cows let off methane gas—lots of it—when they digest food. And methane contributes to global warming.

Studying other planets can teach us about Earth. Mars lost most of its greenhouse gases long ago, leading to much lower temperatures.

Greenhouse gases make the Earth's atmosphere behave like a greenhouse. As in a greenhouse, the Sun's energy passes in, but much of it is trapped inside.

Warming temperatures in the air and in the ocean water have forced many polar bears onto smaller fragments of ice.

Activity: CO₂ Reveal

This experiment shows the power of carbon dioxide, a major greenhouse gas that's pumped into the atmosphere. The ingredients undergo a chemical reaction to produce carbon dioxide. Since it's heavier than air, you can "pour" it out just like water. Ask an adult to help you with the matches.

You will need:

- A small candle
- Matches
- A tablespoon
- Baking soda
- A measuring jug
- A cup
- Vinegar

1. Have a grown-up light the candle and put it at the end of the table or counter.

2. Put 2 tablespoons of baking soda in the jug.

3. Half-fill the cup with vinegar.

4. Slowly pour the vinegar into the jug. The mixture will foam and bubble.

5. Holding one hand over the top of the jug, take it to the candle and tip it slowly over the candle —without actually pouring out the liquid. The flame will be put out by the gas!

You Can Be a Rain Expert

With global temperatures rising, it's even more important for humans to make sure that precious rainwater isn't wasted. Environmental scientists constantly monitor rainfall and look for ways to maintain supplies of water where it's needed most.

It's important to measure how much rain falls in different areas around the world, so changing patterns of weather can be spotted. One of the oldest (and easiest) ways to do this is to check water levels.

Scientists process rainfall information along with data about temperature, time of day and year, and how much water the soil has absorbed.

People in drier parts of the world collect rainwater so that it's not wasted. It can be used to water plants, for washing, and—if filtered—for drinking.

Raindrops are churned around violently within cumulonimbus (thunder) clouds. If they rise high enough, they freeze and form hailstones.

Activity: Make a Rain Gauge

On a warm, sunny day, make a rain gauge with some simple ingredients. A large plastic drinks bottle is ideal, but the bottom usually curves upward. Instead, you need a flat bottom. That's why you need the gelatin dessert—it will set and form a level base.

1. Have an adult nearby for these first two steps. First, ask them to cut across the bottle about two-thirds of the way up.

2. The adult should make up the gelatin dessert in the measuring cup or jug, then pour it into the base of the bottle.

3. Turn the cut-off top part of the bottle upside-down and slide it into the base.

4. Use the ruler to mark a scale along a length of tape that you have positioned on the outside of the bottle.

5. Put the rain gauge outside, well away from buildings or trees that could block the rain.

6. Check the rain gauge every day at the same time, measure the amount of rain collected, and empty the bottle.

You Can Be an Environmentalist

Activists and scientists constantly develop new ways of recycling the mountains of litter that threaten the environment. The problem is global, but experts point out that the solution can start at home.

People once used bottles and containers over and over again. But modern "throwaway" products are creating huge amounts of rubbish.

Environmentalists have promoted the use of family "recycling stations" where items can be sorted according to their material —such as glass, plastic, or paper.

Recycling just one drink can will save enough energy to power a television for 3 hours.

Many communities have special vehicles to collect materials for recycling. Separate compartments are set aside for each type of recycling material.

Activity: Recycling Race

Here's a chance to see who in your family is the recycling champion. Race against your brother, sister, or a parent to see who can sort all of the shopping into the right recycling group the fastest.

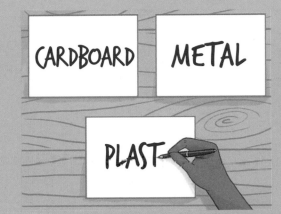

1. Find out which different types of recycling are used in your area—for example metals, paper, cardboard, glass, plastics.

2. Each competitor must write these categories on separate pieces of paper and space those papers across the floor.

3. Ready, set, go! Take each item and put it next to the matching paper label. Whoever has sorted the most items when the shopping bags are empty is the winner.

You Can Be a Botanist

Botanists (plant scientists) study crop growth in different conditions so that they can help the crops flourish. No matter what environment they are in, plants use energy from sunlight and air in a process called photosynthesis.

Rain forests have many layers of plants. But the dense canopy at the top also blocks light from easily reaching the forest floor, where plants struggle more.

Many plants grow in the direction of the light. Some even move through the day as they follow the movement of the Sun across the sky.

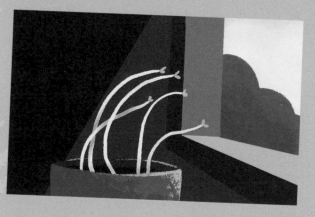

Most plants produce their own food through photosynthesis, but carnivorous (meat-eating) plants also trap and eat insects and spiders.

A dose of light often helps unhealthy plants perk up, unless they've been left too long in the dark.

Activity: Food from Light

You'll soon learn all about the science behind the way plants can create food from light, but would you like some proof of it before your very eyes? Try this demonstration, and you'll see the light.

You will need:

- Black card
- Scissors
- A house plant with large leaves (a geranium is ideal)
- Masking tape
- A clear sandwich bag

1. Cut out two pieces of black paper, each large enough to cover a leaf.

2. Cover the top and bottom of a leaf with the black paper and tape the pieces together.

3. Cover a second leaf, top and bottom, with the sandwich bag and tape it together.

4. Put the plant on a table or windowsill where it will get sunlight.

5. After one week, remove the coverings and observe the shade of the leaves. The "black leaf" will be faded but the other leaf should still be green.

Answers

P. 53 Suspect B wrote the note.

P. 57 1. Brain, 2. Lungs, 3. Heart, 4. Liver, 5. Stomach, 6. Small intestine, 7. Large intestine, 8. Bladder, 9. Skull, 10. Ribs, 11. Spine, 12. Pelvis

P. 59

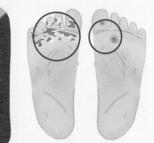

P. 19 A possible solution: "Grip the rightmost cup," "Lift cup three inches," "Move left six inches," "Lower cup and release."

P. 21
1. G   5. F
2. C   6. E
3. A   7. D
4. H   8. B
Note that other solutions are possible.

P. 27 Kavitha's program.

P. 31 The last cog would move clockwise, so the pointer would move down.

P. 39
1. Kazuyo, production architect
2. Julia, landscape architect
3. Frank, design architect
4. Louis, on-site architect

P. 45 You shouldn't include paved-over outdoor spaces, clothes dryers, or coal-burning stoves in your eco-homes.

P. 51 Suspect 3 bit into the chocolate.

P. 61

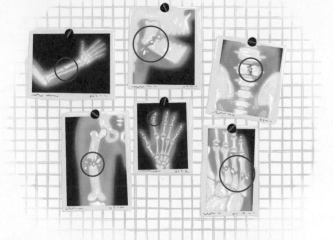

1. Radius (lower arm), 2. Lower jaw, 3. Spine, 4. Femur (thigh bone), 5. Finger, 6. Foot

P. 63
1. DR. WILD   2. DR. BARKING
3. DR. LYONS   4. DR. MUDDI

P. 65

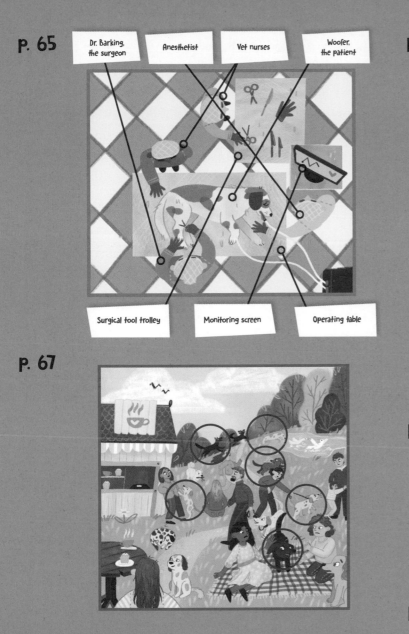

Dr. Barking, the surgeon | Anesthetist | Vet nurses | Woofer, the patient

Surgical tool trolley | Monitoring screen | Operating table

P. 67

P. 69

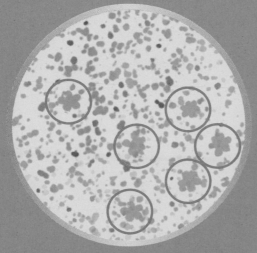

P. 71 Add up the score for your answers, then check your results below.

1. a) 2 b) 1 c) 0   4. a) 1 b) 1 c) 2
2. a) 1 b) 2 c) 0   5. a) 0 b) 2 c) 1
3. a) 1 b) 0 c) 2   6. a) 2 b) 1 c) 0

0–4
Hmmm, you might be better suited to starring in a dinosaur movie!

5–8
If you love dinosaurs and work hard, it could be the career for you.

9–12
Perfect paleontologist potential!

P. 73 Cretaceous: Iguanodon, Spinosaurus, Triceratops, Velociraptor

Jurassic: Allosaurus, Brachiosaurus, Stegosaurus

Triassic: Plateosaurus, Saltopus

P. 75

Glossary

Air current A body of air moving in a definite direction.

Algorithm A set of rules to be followed in order to solve a problem.

Amputate To cut off a body part, such as a leg or tail.

Anemometer An instrument to measure wind speed.

Anesthetist A doctor or vet who makes sure a patient is unable to feel pain during surgery.

Angle The space between two intersecting lines, close to the point where they meet (usually measured in degrees).

Appendicitis An illness that happens when the appendix becomes infected and swollen.

Appendix A small finger-shaped body part attached to the large intestine.

Architect Someone who designs buildings and supervises their construction.

Artificial Made by humans, rather than occurring naturally.

Astronaut A person who is trained to travel in a spacecraft. They are called a cosmonaut if they are from Russia.

Atmosphere The layer of air around the Earth.

Beaufort Scale A scale used to measure wind speeds.

Carbon dioxide A gas produced by respiration (breathing) and by burning organic matter. It is absorbed by plants in photosynthesis, and helps to cause global warming.

Cells Tiny living units that make up the bodies of humans, animals, plants, and other living things.

Chemical Any basic substance that is used in (or produced by) a reaction involving changes to atoms or molecules.

Chemical reaction A change that occurs when two or more substances combine to form a new substance.

Cipher wheel A tool made of two concentric circles, used for making and breaking encrypted messages.

Civil engineer An engineer who concentrates on designing and maintaining roads, railways, bridges, canals, and other structures.

Clicker A gadget that makes a clicking sound, used to help train dogs.

Client Someone for whom a person does a project.

Cog A wheel with a series of teeth on its edge that transfers motion by linking with another cog.

Cord A string-like part used in some robots to make limbs move.

Cretaceous period The latest of the three periods of the Mesozoic era, when dinosaurs lived.

Cumulonimbus A large, puffy cloud that often produces severe thunderstorms.

Cupola The observatory module of the ISS. It has seven windows used for experiments, dockings, and viewing Earth.

Cyclone A swirling windstorm around an area of low air pressure. Also used to mean a tropical cyclone in the Indian or South Pacific Ocean.

Data The information that a computer needs in order to operate.

Decode Convert a coded message into an understandable one.

Diameter The distance of a straight line from side to side passing through the midpoint of a circle.

DNA (deoxyribonucleic acid) The material found in the cells of nearly all living things that controls the growth and work of cells. The instructions contained in DNA are passed down from parents to their children.

Drought A period of very dry weather that can cause water shortages and harm crops.

Eco-friendly Not harmful to the environment or wildlife.

Encode Convert a message into coded form.

Energy The power to make something active.

Engineer Someone who is trained to design and operate machines, engines, or software.

Environment The surroundings, especially natural surroundings or the natural world.

Era A long division of time in the history of the Earth, such as the Mesozoic era.

Evidence Information or materials that prove whether or not something is true. Evidence can be used in a court of law to try to prove the facts about a crime.

Force An influence that produces a physical change or a change in movement.

Forensic scientists Experts who use scientific methods to collect and test evidence in order to solve crimes.

Forging Making a copy of something in order to deceive, or trick.

Formula A rule written with mathematical symbols.

Fossil The remains or trace of a prehistoric living thing, preserved in rock.

Fracture A broken bone.

Fuel A material that is burned to produce heat or power.

Fungi Living things that get their food from rotting material or other living things.

Gear A device, often made of connecting wheels with teeth, that alters the relation between the speed of an engine and other moving parts.

Germ A micro-organism, especially one that causes disease.

Global warming A gradual increase in Earth's average temperature over the last two centuries, caused by human activities.

Greenhouse gases Gases that trap heat in the Earth's atmosphere, leading to global warming.

Habitat The natural home or surroundings of a living thing.

Heat exchanger A machine that uses heat from warm air leaving the building to heat up fresh air coming in.

Heatwave A period of unusually hot weather, normally during the summer.

Hurricane A powerful storm, usually fed by warm ocean water, with destructive winds and enough rainfall to cause serious flooding.

Hydraulic A system that uses fluids or liquids, sealed inside tubes or containers, to put pressure on parts of a machine to make them move.

Industrial To do with making or processing things in factories, or on a large scale.

Infection What happens when germs get inside the body, or a body part.

Insulation The prevention or slowing of the transfer of energy.

Iodine A purplish chemical that is found naturally on Earth.

ISS (International Space Station) An artificial satellite that circles around Earth with astronauts living on board and carrying out scientific experiments.

Jurassic period The middle period of the Mesozoic era, when dinosaurs lived.

Lab Short for laboratory, this is a room or building where scientists do tests or experiments.

Landslide Soil or rocks sliding or slipping down a slope.

Liquid A substance that flows, such as water or milk.

Liver A large body part used for storing and changing body chemicals.

Machine A piece of equipment with several moving parts. It uses power to do a particular type of work.

Mesozoic era The time from about 251 to 66 million years ago, when the dinosaurs lived.

Meteorologist A scientist who studies weather and the atmosphere.

Microgravity Very weak gravity, the kind you would find inside a spacecraft circling around Earth.

Microscope An instrument that uses lenses to view very small objects and living things.

Molecule A group of atoms that are bonded together. They form what is known as a chemical compound. A molecule is the smallest particle that still has all the chemical properties of the substance.

Monitor To observe something or someone closely.

Motor A device that turns fuel or electricity into motion, usually rotating motion, to make a moving part of a machine work.

Operation Another name for surgery.

Organs Body parts that have particular jobs to do, such as the brain, stomach, or heart.

Oxygen A gas that is essential for life. It is part of the atmosphere and is used for respiration. It is produced by plants in photosynthesis.

Paleontology The study of fossils and what they reveal about prehistoric life.

Pelvis The large bone that connects the spine to the lower or back legs.

Pendulum A weight hung from a fixed point, so it can swing freely.

Period A division of time that is shorter than an era.

Photosynthesis The chemical process that enables plants to use sunlight to convert carbon dioxide (a gas found in air) and water into food.

Planet A world, orbiting a star that has enough mass and gravity to pull itself into a ball-like shape and clear space around it of other large objects.

Polygon A 2-D shape with straight sides.

Program A set of instructions that tells a robot or other computerized device how to carry out a task.

Programming language A language made up of a set of commands, symbols, and rules, used for writing programs for robots and computers.

Pulse A rhythmic throbbing that can be felt in the arteries as the heart beats and pushes blood through them.

PVC (polyvinyl chloride) A type of strong plastic sometimes used to make window frames.

Rain gauge A device that measures the amount of rainfall.

Recycling Finding ways of reusing rather than throwing away products.

Renewable Able to be replaced, so it doesn't get used up.

Resource Any substance that is useful for human life.

Right angle An angle of 90° (e.g., the corner of a square, or a quarter of a circle).

Rocket A vehicle that drives itself forward through a controlled chemical explosion and can therefore travel in the vacuum of space.

Rotation Movement around a central point or axis.

Sample A small part of a substance, often used for testing.

Scytale A cylindrical tool used for making and breaking codes.

Seismograph An instrument that measures and records details of motion in the ground, such as earthquakes and volcanic eruptions.

Seismoscope An instrument that responds to motion in the ground, such as those caused by earthquakes and volcanic eruptions.

Software The programs and other operating data used by a computer.

Solar panel A panel of material that turns energy from sunlight into a flow of electricity.

Solar System The eight planets (including Earth) and their moons, and other objects such as asteroids, that orbit around the Sun.

Solid Firm and keeping a distinct shape.

Space probe A robotic spacecraft that explores space without any crew on board.

Speed The rate at which something moves.

Splint A rigid object used to hold a body part still to allow a broken bone to heal.

Star An astronomical body that generates light and other energy. It is made of gas and dust.

Surgeon A doctor or vet who carries out surgery, or operations.

Surgery (noun) A name for the building where a doctor or vet works.

Surgery (verb) Working on a patient's insides to fix, mend, replace, or treat a body part.

Suspect A person thought to be possibly guilty of a crime.

Suspension bridge A bridge for which the weight of the deck is supported by vertical cables attached to other cables that run between towers.

Sustainability Using natural resources in such a way that they won't run out in the future.

Teach pendant A device attached to some types of robot that allows engineers or users to key in instructions or simple programs.

Technician Someone who works with specialist machines or equipment.

Technology The use of scientific knowledge to develop machinery and equipment.

Tendon A string-like part that pulls on body parts to make them move; found in living things and in robots.

Territory The area that an animal marks out or guards as its own.

Thrust The force produced by a rocket engine that pushes the spacecraft forward.

Tornado A powerful windstorm that forms a narrow spiral or funnel of whirling air.

Tremor A quivering movement in the ground, especially following earthquakes and volcanic eruptions.

Triassic period The earliest of the periods of the Mesozoic era, when dinosaurs lived.

Unique Unlike anything else.

Universe All of space and everything in it.

Veins Blood vessels that carry blood toward the heart from other body parts.

Veterinary To do with animal medicine. "Vet" is short for veterinary surgeon.

Virtual reality A space created by a computer that resembles the "real world" in sight and sound.

Viruses Micro-organisms that can only reproduce (by making copies of themselves) inside the cells of other living things. Viruses can cause illness.

Waterspout A small windstorm similar to a tornado that forms over water.

Weather balloon A type of balloon with measuring devices on it that is released into the sky to measure weather conditions.

Weather satellite A human-made satellite orbiting the Earth, used to capture images of weather patterns or record weather information.

Weather station A building or device that measures many different aspects of the weather.

Welding Fixing metal parts together by heating them so that they melt together.

Wildfire A fire that is burning out of control across a large area, especially in the wilderness or countryside.

X-ray A type of photo that can show a person's or animal's insides.

Index